A LITTLE TALK WITH JAMAICA - AS LONG AS I LIVE

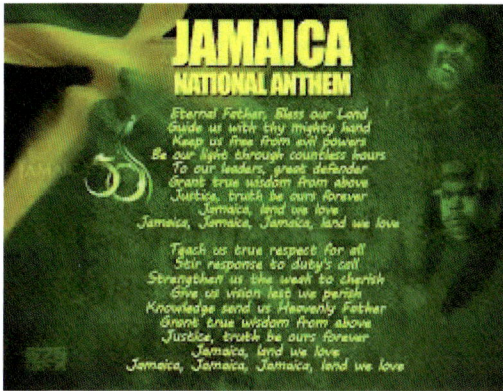

As long as I live Jamaica I will remember you. You will always be in my thoughts, my hope and dreams. You are the land of my birth and I will forever ever cherish you and ask God - Good God and Allelujah to bless you - remember you also. You will never be forgotten because I truly love you, truly love your land as well as truly thank God and Good God for allowing me to be born in you.

Jamaica you will always be of my true and good world - good and true will. You will always be a part of my good and true universe. You are a part of my heart of goodness and I am truly glad Good God and God gave me you.

Michelle Jean

As long as I live, I will never forget you
You are heaven sent
The truth in my world
My truthful thoughts

As long as I live, I will remember the times we had. Special are they hence they are dear to me.

As I hold you close to my heart, I will always remember the good and bad times

The pain
Tears
Your beautiful smile

As long as I live, I will remember you.

Michelle Jean

Without truth we are nothing and as I write this book and listen to A Better Way by Jah Cure, I have to think of you Jamaica.

I have to think of what you've become due to the evils of man - your own people.

Good and bad times we've had and now Jamaica is no more.

We gave you up because we could not be true; we held on to death and now it's too late for you.

My hope is gone and or fading for you.

How can I continue to plea for you without losing my soul - place with God - Good God?

I can no longer piss off death because death wants you Jamaica, due to the vile and wicked ways of your people.

Soon destruction will be on land and it is disheartening to know what will happen to millions of you.

I must give instructions to death and you are included in this instruction. Yes it's hard because I've seen the flag of life taken from you and given to death and this is sad.

Jamaica has lost life and it's unfortunate that we made this happen.

We gave up life for death and there is nothing I can do to save you. I've tried but failed, hence I was not to save you. I cannot save sin's children because in all you the people of Jamaica did, you forgot about truth - Good God and your true name.

YOU FORGOT THAT JAMAICA MEANS GOD MADE ME HENCE THE NAME JA-MAI-CA.

You forgot that in all that you do that is sinful - evil, there is a price to pay.

You forgot about the wages of sin and now not even I can save you nor do I truly want to. However, if I can save the land I will, but I will not take away from death's pay. We all knew what we were doing and instead of saving self, we gave land and people over to death.

Death is real and they will be at your doorstep real soon.

Soon they will be knocking at your doors and you will be sorry because you kept the order of death.

You feasted with death.

Made sacrifices unto death.

Gave your lives over to death, hence in all that you give death, death must take.

Death must claim their own hence death must take you Jamaica. Like Israel - the Israelites in the book of sin it said, "WOE BE UNTO THE JEWS THAT CALL THEMSELVES

JEWS BECAUSE THEY ARE OF THE SYNAGOGUE OF SATAN."

Ethiopians are the original Jews but they were not of God - Good God. They were the Ethers - people of the gaseous clouds - Luciferians hence humanity truly do not know about Lucy and where she came from but now they know.

Eve - Evening was not of the Garden of Eden, hence tales embedded in the Book of Sin by the White Jews and the many writers thereof.

In all Good God has tried he too has failed because you the people of Jamaica failed him. You do not listen hence you serve man and worship man. Saying these men are our gods but yet do not know that God - Good God and Life cannot die he can only live.

Things you do not know you take up and say it is yours. Some of you go as far as killing others for your beliefs and that is sad.

We knew of the Careless Ethiopians but none of you listened to the truths handed down to us.

We accepted the Ethiopian way from start to finish and now look at land and people.

We betrayed God - Good God because we take up lies - the lies of the Babylonians and say it is our truth, history and heritage when we know of ourselves it was and is not ours nor is it ours to keep.

We say down with Babylon and Babylon must fall but yet praise and worship a known Babylonian - Selassie.

We practice the Babylonian way and say Babylon is evil but yet we do as Babylon - the Babylonians.

How does that work Jamaica?

Yes our language and heritage was taken from us but we were the ones to give up all to be a part of the Babylonian world and system of things.

They lied to us and enslaved us.

They took our lands including culture, peaceful way of life, hope, truths and now look at us; fighting for lifestyles that do not belong to us.

We keep fighting for a culture that is not of us.

We fight for rites and customs that are not of us.

We keep fighting for people that are not of us.

We keep fighting for a language that is not of us.

We keep fighting to marry people that are not of us; people that are forbidden to us to marry because they are not our own.

We keep fighting for gods and or deities that is not of us and for us.

<u>All this and more we do and now look at us; on the chopping block of death literally.</u>

We had many warning signs but we ignored them.

We had many messengers and we slandered and killed them.

We had the protection of Good God and we gave that up including selling him out for dirty pieces of silver.

Now truly look at us because soon all we will have is our memory of a land and people that was but was not.

Duly remember our asking in our National Anthem and Pledge.

The Jamaican National Anthem
Eternal Father bless our land,
Guard us with Thy Mighty Hand,
Keep us free from evil powers,
Be our light through countless hours.
To our Leaders, Great Defender,
Grant true wisdom from above.
Justice, Truth be ours forever,
Jamaica, Land we love.
Jamaica, Jamaica, Jamaica land we love.

Teach us true respect for all,
Stir response to duty's call, strengthen us
the weak to cherish,
Give us vision lest we perish.
Knowledge send us Heavenly Father,
Grant true wisdom from above.
Justice, Truth be ours forever,
Jamaica, land we love.
Jamaica, Jamaica, Jamaica land we love.

All this we asked Good God for and he did grant us our prayer and asking, but instead of accepting his true gifts, we rejected all the goodness he Good God has and have given us.

He gave us knowledge and vision but we abandoned his knowledge and vision. We accepted the devil's way hence the many churches on the island by the different denominations of sin and deceit.

He gave us visions because many of us know the truth of death - the dead, life and many more.

He gave us justice but instead of leading by example and treat each other with respect, we pervert the course of justice.

Many rape and get away with it including politicians.

Many kill and get away with it including politicians, entertainers and ordinary citizens.

Many sell children - child trafficking.

<u>Many hate and kill others due to sexual orientation. But yet the foundation and framework of your churches, including your holy book - the bible is based on nastiness - incest, adultery, murder, theft, lies and deceit.</u>

In your nasty and holy book of sin, fathers can lay with daughters and it's okay - you are okay with this. (Adam and Eve)

In your nasty and holy book of sin, brothers can lay with sister and it's okay - you are okay with this. (Abraham and Sarah)

In your nasty and holy book of sin, men can go to war and kill - take lands and people (lives) that don't belong to them and it's okay - you are okay with this. (The many so called prophets - warmongers that kill and steal.)

Every commandment you break but yet say you love and praise God - Good God.

Every vile act known to man is listed in the book of sin – man's book, but yet none of you have looked into this.

None of you say wait a minute, this is wrong. This could not be of God – Good God.

Hence as human's we are so hypocritical because we say incest is wrong and it is infinitely and indefinitely wrong, but yet we condone it and say it is right just because it's in the bible.

What makes the bible correct?

Did God = Good God write it?

No he did not.

So how can we say the bible is his book when the framework and foundation of this book is wrong - deceitful?

National Pledge

Before God and all mankind, I pledge the love and loyalty of my heart, the wisdom and courage of my mind, the strength and vigour of my body in the service of my fellow citizens; I promise to stand up for Justice, Brotherhood and Peace, to work diligently and creatively, to think generously and honestly, so that Jamaica may, under God, increase in beauty, fellowship and prosperity, and play her part in advancing the welfare of the whole human race.

Now tell me how many have kept this pledge?

We could not honour our pledge hence we lied before God – Good God and Man - Humanity.

This was our pledge of truth to Good God but yet we abandoned this; our pledge –

truth. _So how can God - Good God trust us_
IF WE BREAK OUR PLEDGE TO HIM TIME
AND TIME AGAIN?

HOW CAN OR COULD GOOD GOD BUILD
HIS HOME IN JAMAICA - A LAND THAT
CANNOT HONOUR THEIR VOW OF TRUTH
UNTO HIM?

How can he Good God built his good
foundation (s) and framework (s) with us
and in us if every commandment of
goodness and truth we break?

We failed God - Good God because we were
never truthful to him. He gave us
goodness but we abandoned that
goodness and truth for all that is
unclean - dirty and now land and people
have been deemed unclean - dirty in the
eyes and sight of God - Good God.

We could not honour our pledge hence the
flag of life has been taken from you and
handed over to death.

We gave up life for death hence Jamaica is the way it is. No truth hath you hence death walks the land daily and take one by one and two by two.

<u>WE MADE A PLEDGE AND COULD NOT KEEP IT hence our marriage vow has been broken literally.</u>

Yes marriage vow because your pledge was your union and marriage to Good God and you broke it, could not honour it hence YOU CHEATED ON GOD - GOOD GOD WITH DEATH.

You were adulterers and now Good God have abandoned you; meaning divorced you and took his flag - truth from you.

<u>YOUR VOW YOU COULD NOT KEEP BECAUSE NONE OF YOU WERE CLEAN.</u>

Good God kept his vow but you could not keep your vow hence your divorce decree - DEATH.

Yes it's sad but it's life; the way you wanted it to be.

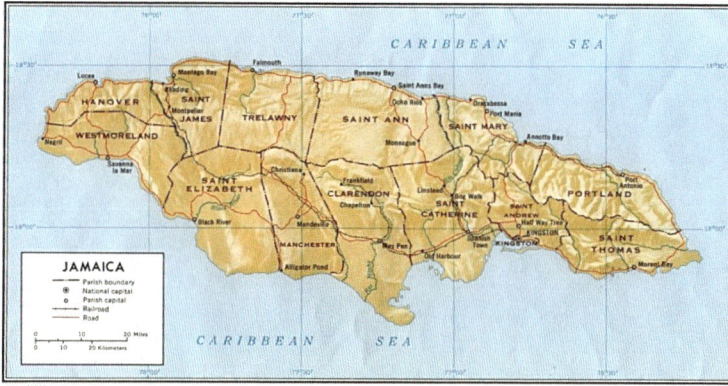

In all that you did, you chose death all around. None of you saw this, but truly look at the Jamaican coat of arms and see what you chose as your head.

Look to the right and left side of the coat of arms.

Now look at the center. Yes the cross of death but for all who have an eye will see that the cross is inverted. Hence death has always been on the land of Jamaica. We gave ourselves over to be possessed by demons. Hence demons walk the land and possess at will - kill. We chose the cross of death as our center of life and a gator as our head. So how can God - Good God save us when we give all to death including our souls?

So now tell me Jamaica, how can Good God build his home and kingdom in you when you've chosen death for yourself all around?

Michelle Jean.

It's funny how we say we pree life but yet hold up the flag of death.

It's funny how we say we pree life but yet go to whore houses (churches) and pay for death as well as pay for death to take us - kill us.

Wow.

Good God gave us wisdom but in all that we do, we've given up wisdom to live like fools - clowns in the devil's court houses.

We do not care about life hence when Germany burned the Flag of Life Jamaica did nothing.

The government did not defend Good God, nor did the millions of people. So as you take away life, life must be taken from you and has been taken from you.

All that you have you will lose because none of you defend God - Good God. And you the Rastas' dare not say we've kept true to life because you've all kept true to Lucifer. Hence many of you say you are of the order of Melchesidec.

YOU KNOW NOTHING, HENCE ALL OF YOU GLOBALLY HAVE AND HAS KEPT THE ORDER OF DEATH AND NOT THE ORDER OF LIFE. HENCE NONE OF YOU KNOW LIFE BECAUSE YOU ARE ALL OF THE ORDER OF THE DEAD – DEATH.

Duly remember the death angels and their hair. You wear the clown of glory of death on your heads hence dreadlocks; the grateful and dreadful dead.

Your hair is the hair of death hence the order of death was kept by you.

Yes you are all dead because all you know is death.

You say Babylon must fall but yet know not that you praise a Babylonian.

You pree Ethiopia without knowing Ethiopia sold out Good God and Allelujah long before Eve (Evening) hence Ethiopia was mentioned in the book of sin - man's dirty book that they call holy.

You are all lies hence you sing about lies and worship lies - Selassie High because you say this Luciferian is your God, hence the Rastafarian Nations of Lies Globally.
There is no difference between you and the deceitful Babylonians of death because you uphold the practices of death and truly don't even know it.

You all fall under the ORDER OF ISLAM BECAUSE YOU ARE THE ONES LEADING GOOD GOD'S CHILDREN TO THE SLAUGHTER HOUSE WITH YOUR LIES.

YOU WILLINGLY EMBRACE BABYLON AND SAY BABYLON MUST FALL WITHOUT KNOWING THAT YOU TOO ARE BABYLONIANS HENCE YOU ALL MUST FALL.

You talk about Babylon but yet HAVE NOT TRUTH OF YOUR HISTORY, HERITAGE, LANGUAGE, CULTURE AND LAND.

You talk about Babylon and sing about Babylon but yet know not that you are spreading lies and telling lies. Hence you teach your children lies.

YOU SING AGAINST YOUR OWN (BABYLON) BUT YET ACCEPT THEIR TEACHINGS, WAY OF LIFE, LANGUAGE, LIES AND DECEIT.

You sing about your own but yet know not that you are like unto a double edged sword that cuts this way and that way with your tongues.

And you the Christians do not blame Rastas for all because you are no different from them either.

You say you are but yet are not. Not one of you can save humanity with your religion - lies.

Look at the different religions of earth but yet none can speak the truth or save any of you.

Yes the Rastas kept the order of death but you tell lies on Good God himself as well as keep the order of death. You say you must die to see Good God but yet in your book of sin Job saw Good God and lived. He did not die so where did death come into play? I've seen Good God and I did not die. He allowed me to see him in the image that my eyes can perceive. And don't go there with image because I know the lots of you deceiving vipers.

Live good and clean, truthful and honest and he Good God will show you him in earth and in the spiritual realm.

You the Christians write books of lies and spread lies saying God - Good God sent his only begotten son to die for you.

Bitches you sin and My Beloved should send his child to die for a bunch of sinful vipers that live dirty - unclean?

Bitch you're unclean. Good God cannot save you because YOU BELIEVE IN DEATH AND LIVE FOR DEATH. NOT ONE OF YOU LIVE FOR LIFE SO WHY SHOULD LIFE - GOOD LIFE - ALLELUJAH AND GOOD GOD SAVE ANY OF YOU?

You do nothing for him but expect him to do all for you. Well it cannot work because "THE WAGES OF SIN IS DEATH **BUT TRUTH IS EVERLASTING LIFE.** So if you have not truth you cannot have everlasting life.

You trust in the lies of men - the clergy but yet the clergy and all their lies cannot save you.

You trust the clergy of your church so much that none of you know that you are hell bound indefinitely.

PEOPLE THE CHURCH TELL LIES ON GOD - GOOD GOD AND YOU FOLLOW THIS LIE HENCE YOU WILL NOT BE SAVED ON EARTH NOR WILL YOU BE SAVED IN THE GRAVE.

Wow, lies told on Good God - Allelujah is a grave sin and I so don't want to be any of you right now. Wow, have mercy Lord because they truly don't know.

Jamaica you truly don't know.

You asked for it all (goodness) and Good God gave it all to you and you snaked him like that?

No for real, you snaked Good God like that. You were the rat to deceive him like that in this modern day and time.

Your book of sin talks about the vileness of sin but I never thought I would find this in you, the people of Jamaica and the world. The global meat market of sin and deceit.

Take a look at the murders on the island, the vile murders where men and women are beheaded.

Take a look at the corruption of Government and Police including some of the people.

Take a look at the child trafficking on the island.

Take a look at the countless murders of babies.

Take a look at the raping and murdering of young girls.

Take a look at the churches and how you buy into their lies and deceit thinking you are going to go to heaven when the heaven that they give you is hell.

You pay for hell but could not see your own wrongs - evils.

Like I've said before, if the churches globally could save humanity, how come humanity is slated to die before 2032?

Many of you are saying you are going to live forever, but yet none of you are clean.

You say you are clean but yet you cut down your next door neighbour.

You say you are clean but yet you deceive.

You say you are clean but yet have affairs on your wife and or husband.

You say you are clean but yet have no truth of God - Good God and Allelujah.

You say you are clean but yet steal it all from your sister and brother including friends and colleagues even kill them.

You say you are clean but yet steal it all from your parents even kill them.

You say you love God but yet take it all from God including you.

You say you love God but yet give him all that is dirty and kill the goodness of earth in the process of it all.

So how can any of us be saved when we are truly not clean.

So Jamaica as long as I live I will think of you and what you have done to yourself.

You will be a testament to man - humanity of what we should not be and or become. When God - Good God gives you something truthfully, you are to keep it and cherish it as well as take care of it because you asked for it and it was well given.

He Good God gave you goodness and instead of receiving this goodness and truth, you turned your backs on it - walked away from it.

__To you it was not good enough, but it was more than good enough because all that was given unto you was given by Good God and it was given true.__

If you do not receive Good God how can he help you?

How can he continue to maintain and sustain you if you gave him up for death?

How can he continue to reside with you if you keep accepting and receiving death?

How can he continue to maintain and sustain you if you cannot be truthful and good to him - honest?

How can he set up his kingdom in you if you are unclean?

Like I've said, all the lands of God - Good God gave unto his children they gave it up and has failed him. Now he has to pass you over as you've passed him over.

We constantly refuse to pass over death, so death comes now to enslave and inflict pain - true pain because this is what you said you wanted.

NONE OF YOU COULD WAIT.

NONE OF YOU COULD GIVE UP DEATH.

NONE OF YOU COULD GIVE UP SLAVERY.

NONE OF YOU COULD GIVE UP PAIN.

So as you accepted and received death, death must take you to hell with him and give you all your heart's desire.

You did not want or need truth. So now hell must receive you in goodness and in truth because you lived your life for death and pain- the demons of hell.

You did not live for life hence the massive killings on the island.

Think about it. Jamaica became the murder capitol of the world hence we disrespected the name of God - Good God. We show humanity globally that we cannot be trusted and we are giver backer takers that live by lies and spew lies. We made a pledge to Allelujah and Good God but could not honour it. Hence as Jamaicans none of you are of God - Good God because none of you knew that Jah is a part of Allelujah just as Allah is a part of Allelujah. And if any of us were clean we would hold Allelujah true to us and live clean and good - truthful and honest at all times.

You Jamaica had the flag of life - the physical flag of life and you let it go. You handed your life over to death because death has the flag of life. But death cannot hold on to the flag of life because good and true life belongs not to death. I reclaim and claim the flag of life in the name of Good God and Allelujah and hand back the true and good flag of Jamaica back to Good God in his wonderful and precious name. Death cannot hold life down hence I receive the goodness and truth of Good God on his behalf.

Death can take you his evil people but death cannot have or take the flag of life. His Good God's children - true and righteous children are governed by life and the flags of life not just in the physical realm but in the spiritual realm also.

No Jamaica, I do not do this for your people, I truly do this for Good God because he's my keep and I will truly live by his pledge of truth. Hence I will stand before him Good God and Man and tell him of my truth and good will towards him and all that he's given me. In all that I do, I will do my best not fail him. I have to be grateful to him and stand in truth and goodness with him because he does truly care about all of us. We are the ones that truly do not care about him. We are the ungrateful ones that forgot about his goodness and kindness in all that he's given us. Trust me any how he (Good God and Allelujah) make me fail, or let evil cloud my sight, we will have it out because he's my earthly, universal and spiritual protector, father and truth. He's also my mother that guides me and holds me down when I'm not to walk on a certain path.

As humans we fail to see the goodness of Good God but I cannot fail to see it. Hence I have to reclaim life - The Jamaican Flag from death and put it firmly in the hands and or possession of good life, truth, goodness, cleanliness, honesty and that good life, truth, goodness, cleanliness and honesty is Good God and Allelujah. He is my good will hence death cannot take the Jamaican flag because this flag does not belong to him. His people belong to him and I have to leave him and his people alone. Death has no claim to life, but death have claim to many of you because you are not of life but of death. Hence you do deadly things.

I refuse to let sins wicked and evil people take life - the flag of life and hand it over willingly to death. Come on now.

Who are they to do this?

Who are they to take what do not rightfully belong to them?

They have no shame because their women and men are like unto Delilah that go round and round like merry-go-rounds; hence the whoredom that they do daily.

Men and woman are like service jockeys that go this and that furlong in holes (vaginas) and a top sticks (penises) for pleasure. They know not the sacredity of sex - pleasure not just in the exchange of fluids but in touch; feel.

The woman and young girls hath no shame and pride in themselves because the more than vulgar and vile dance hall fraternity spread nastiness not just amongst themselves but amongst their children. Hence many grow up with no values and pride. Mama and Daddy had none now children have none.

Daddy and Mommy whore worse than the demons of hell - no, yes because the demons of hell live for pain and the more you sin is the more pain they inflict on you, hence SLAVERY OF OLD AND SOON TO BE SHORTLY.

Young girls grow up without values because men can use cell phones to buy them. Meaning get them to open their legs and the man come in and take what he wants whilst leaving her pregnant.

Some man dey with mother and daughter at the same time, not to mention aunts and cousins.

Some use the internet as their playing ground hence the new form of prostitution literally.

That's not all because mothers use their children as hand carts; meaning let people pay their children to go beg money in the streets for pay.

Some mothers give politicians access to their kids because child trafficking happens in Jamaica on a regular basis.

Politicians extort business people for money and if they do pay up they are killed. Hence no politician globally can say they are going to see the King - Good God and Allelujah because they have no values nor do they keep his commandments literally.

People work Obeah and do all manner of evil to keep the next person down but yet they say they worship and praise God.

Many fathers lay with their children and impregnate them whist the wife sit there and turn a blind eye to her husband's nastiness. Hence her nastiness as well as she condoning nastiness literally.

Many say they go to church and serve God but yet spend their money on oil a bring back, oil a kip man, oil a kip oman; oil a kip gal, oil a get job, oil a fire principal because drangcrow let go inna school, oil a bring customers to your business, oil a put pickney thru school, oil a win contest; oil a win political seat in office; oil a raise di dead fi kill di next man; oil a don't ketch mi when mi teef; oil a win di case inna court. You name it, many of you do it and more including have di oil a ketch man.

Trust me many is going to cry out for death and death will not come because the demons have them under lock and key. None of you know pain because like I've said, the demons of hell truly love pain and they live for pain. Let me tell you something. We say some men are sadistic to the way they inflict pain before they kill. Trust me this is nothing compared to the pain these demon will inflict on you. Like I've told you in my other books the flesh does not feel pain, the spirit does. So learn from what the spirit is trying to tell you because at the end of the day, it's your life and no one is going to save you in the grave.

Hell's fire will be real to many soon and trust me all who cry out and say, God why have though forsaken me will find out that they were the ones to forsake God – Good God with their lies and unclean nature – ways.

We do not bring up our children to have good and true values.

We do not bring up our children to respect others including self and Good God.

And no by going to church does not make you clean, it makes you sinful – of the children of death. Hence you were told in Revelations that you are THE FIRST BEGOTTEN OF THE DEAD. Meaning you are DEATH'S CHILDREN BECAUSE YOU

LIVE TO DIE. WE CANNOT FORGET WHAT SOME OF OUR PARENTS DID. THEY HANDED SOME OF YOU OVER TO DEATH VIA BAPTISM AND OR CHRISTENINGS.

Good values have we not because we parade around like children of the lost and not children of the wise.

You parade around thinking that you are better than the next man but in truth you are not better but the same. Like the next sinful and deceitful person.

Look at Jamaica; a beautiful paradise that Good God separated from all and you've turned the island into the modern day Sodom and Gomorrah.

Sodom and Gomorrah was destroyed because the place was that unclean and now Jamaica was deemed unclean by Good God and death wants the island and people so bad and or that badly.

I will not stand in death's way again but I will take back the flag of life from death. This flag belongs not to death but to Good God. I will hold the flag of life in glory because this flag is within me hence Good God resides in me. He is my good and true house - home and I have to be his good and true house - home also.

What belongs to death, death must take because I have to step aside and let death ravish and destroy.

Death's people do not belong to God - Good God hence I must leave them alone. I will not commission death not to take his people because they truly belong to him. I will however commission death to leave the true children and people - family of Good God alone.

You cannot ask for goodness and when you get it Frunze upon it.

You cannot tell Good God the goodness he's given you is not good enough.

You cannot tell Good God that yu nuh want him after you specifically asked for him and his blessings.

You cannot tell Good God that death gives better things than him because death does not give anything but death.

Death cannot create, death can only kill. Come on now.

Unnu get paradise and destroy paradise.

Unnu get di name of Good God and unnu lie and deceive under and in the name of God - Good God.

Unnu ha wey the global community want and unnu frig it up. Hence ole people sey wanti wanti caane get eee and getti getti no want eee.

SO SINCE NONE OF YOU WANTED THE GOODNESS OF GOOD GOD, IT MUST BE TAKEN FROM YOU AND IT HAS BEEN TAKEN FROM YOU LITERALLY.

YOU COMMITTED YOURSELVES TO DEATH LITERALLY and now death must collect his and her pay.

Like I've said, many of you are going to die of hunger and starvation.

Many of you are going to die of medical want and need.

Many of you are going to die because of lack of drinking water - food.

Many of you are going to die more by the hands of your fellow men and woman because you will not be able to import and export (buy and sell). And if any country in the global community disobey the will of Good God and Allelujah their fate will be worse than yours. Death by disobedience because they did disobey the will of Good God. Hence disobedience is not just a sin but death also.

Many of you are going to cry out for Jesus and Jesus will not save you because NO ONE CAN CHANGE THE WORD AND WILL OF GOD - GOOD GOD WHEN IT COMES TO YOUR LAND. HE GOOD GOD SAID SPECIFICALLY THAT, "JAMAICA IS DIRTY - UNCLEAN." So everyone in the international community must heed and obey the words of Good God and leave Jamaica and its people alone to your own demise; death. Anyone breaks this law then death must be instructed to leave your land barren and without food and water for interfering in the course of death - his taking.

Jamaicans knew better but instead of heeding the warnings from the sinking of Port Royal and the different hurricanes and small earthquakes they've gotten; they sinned more vile and wicked in and under the name of Good God.

<u>You the people of Jamaica caused Good God to deem your land unclean hence not one of his (Good God's) children can go into the land because we are forbidden to do so.</u>

To go against God - Good God and go into the land of Jamaica is automatic death for them. However if you do not believe in God - Good God then you are not included in this.

Dirty and unclean can go into Jamaica if it be their will. But if I were you, I would not because there is death and then there's a greater death - hotter death so truly think. I will not send you there hence I am warning you not to go.

So Jamaica truly good luck to many of you. Some of you follow some of these dancehall artists to a tee and think that your actions will not be a reflection on you.

Yes Ninja Man I liked you but you sold out hence you are now worried about your incarceration. Let me tell you this, an innocent man worries not about guilt, but a guilty man worries about his guilt, incarceration.

If you are of Good God and true, then Good God will protect you and take you out of the mess and evil wicked people set you in.

Many a unnu sey unnu pree God but yet live by the sword of death. Meaning unnu kill an sey unnu no do it. YES THE SYSTEM OF MEN WAS SET UP TO PROTECT THE WICKED. WICKED AND EVIL PEOPLE THAT THINK THEY ARE ABOVE THE LAW. WICKED AND EVIL PEOPLE THAT KILL. WICKED AND EVIL PEOPLE THAT PERVERT THE COURSE OF JUSTICE IN ALL THAT THEY DO HENCE SOME A UNNU GET OFF DUE TO BACK DOOR DEALINGS. Politicians, lawyers, jurors, judge, police man and women including di wanga jut dem wey call demself citizens pay off in the form of dem belly - food.

Good hath nothing to do with the systems of men because Good do not live to go to court nor do they live or for the injustice of man.

Good do not live to lie and deceive.

Good does not kill.

In all that good is trying to do, good is trying to separate from evil because evil sucks the life out of you and kill you in the process - end.

Many a unnu ha more dan bag a pickney (children) and can't mind them or share your love of truth with them.

Many of them go hungry - unfed and unnu sey unnu a pree God an a go gaah heaven. Wait a hell unnu a go guh because sey unnu abandon unnu pickney dem.

Unnu whore like if not worse than Solomon and ha pickney yahso and dehso. Now let me ask you this; do you truly think Good God favours you?

Whoredom is a sin. You are not to have children you cannot support and or give true love to. Hence no child is guaranteed to save any of us upon death. Come on now.

We do wrongs and say we are right when we know we are wrong.

How many a unnu tek money from people a foreign and in the same Jamaica dey and kill?

How many lives have some of you taken for money and sport?

Men and Women send unnu money from foreign fi kill an unnu willingly tek it an kill whist sinking the island further into debt with death.

Politicians sell unnu including children and unnu think it's a good thing, meaning unnu cover up things.

Some of the people live in less than humane conditions because nuff a unnu treat unnu hog dem better than the way the government treat unnu. And unnu wonder why Jamaica cannot be better. Like I've said, not one of you thought about the consequences of our actions - sins.

Well our evils reach that point in time where hell will now come down to earth and devour the lots of you literally.

HENCE NONE OF YOU CAN BLAME ANYONE BUT SELF.

You ignored the warnings signs hence you were told by Bob Marley in TIME WILL TELL. Jah gave unnu di power - the flag of life and unnu dash eee way. Now paradise will turn into hell shortly literally.

None of you wanted life nor did you want truth for self and land.

It's amazing how Good God and Allelujah have given every black nation true life and riches beyond our imagination and we gave it up for naught.

All that he Good God and Allelujah has and have given us including self we hand it over to death literally.

What makes death so precious that we have to give all to him including self?

We could not keep his goodness and his trust. So tell me if Good God and Allelujah cannot trust us to keep his order, who can?

Truth is the key to life and if you cannot live true, you cannot have life nor will you get it.

WELL TIME A TELL NOW HENCE THE TIME OF DEATH FOR ALL OF YOU THAT IS EVIL – UNTRUE.

DULY REMEMBER YOUR NATIONAL ANTHEM AND NATIONAL PLEDGE AND TELL GOOD GOD WHY YOU AS A NATION AND PEOPLE FAILED HIM.

Your time is up Jamaica and hell comes to take his and her own – YOU.

Michelle Jean

JAMAICA TO DI WURL

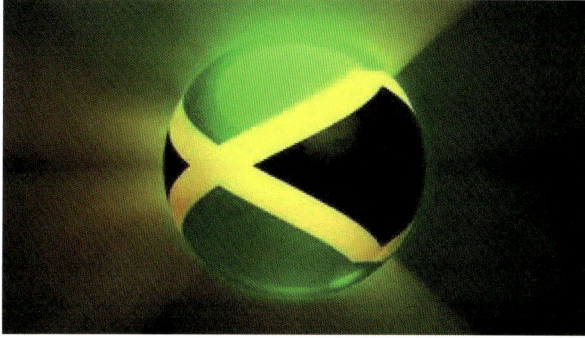

THE BEAUTY OF PARADISE

Robert Nesta Marley

Marcus Mosiah Garvey

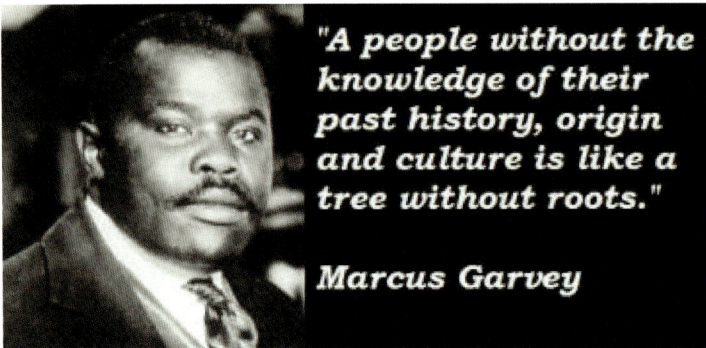

"A people without the knowledge of their past history, origin and culture is like a tree without roots."

Marcus Garvey

"If you have no confidence in self, you are twice defeated in the race of life."

Marcus Garvey

"The Black skin is not a badge of shame, but rather a glorious symbol of national greatness."

Marcus Garvey

"There is no force like success, and that is why the individual makes all effort to surround himself throughout life with the evidence of it; as of the individual, so should it be of the nation."

Marcus Garvey

"God and Nature first made us what we are, and then out of our own created genius we make ourselves what we want to be. Follow always that great law. Let the sky and God be our limit and Eternity our measurement."

Marcus Garvey

We are going to emancipate ourselves from mental slavery because whilst others might free the body, none but ourselves can free the mind.

MARCUS GARVEY SPEAKING IN MENELIK HALL, SYDNEY, NOVA SCOTIA 1937

Sam Sharpe

Sam Sharpe was enslaved on both the Croydon Plantation and at a property in Montego Bay in Saint James. He was owned by Samuel Sharpe, Esquire, Attorney. He was a man of exceptional intelligence, and a Baptist lay preacher. He believed all men were created in the image of God, were equal, and that therefore slavery was wrong. He preached about the injustices of slavery and read of the works of the abolitionists.

In 1831 Sharpe organized a passive resistance movement against slavery in St. James, Trelawny and Westmoreland by demanding pay for work done. Set to begin during Christmas 1831 the strike turned into an armed rebellion. The uprising was savagely suppressed by the English. Hundreds of enslaved people were caught, tried and executed in the Montego Bay market place on May 23, 1832.

However, the widespread nature and seriousness of the Rebellion convinced the British Government that the time had come to end the enslavement of African people. This took place on August 1, 1834 and therefore Sam Sharpe had not died in vain.

Sam Sharpe was buried under the pulpit of the Burchell Baptist Church, here in Montego Bay. In recognition of his fight for freedom, Sam Sharpe has been declared one of Jamaica's National Heroes. This monument is dedicated to Sam Sharpe, National Hero, and shows him preaching to his people.

SAM SHARPE (DIED) 1832

PAUL BOGLE

Nanny

Jamaican Food

None of us can say Good God did not give us all that we needed and we let him down.

We let our heroes down; heroes that fought for us - our land and freedom.

Look at Jamaica now; in debt to everyone.

- *We had the man that told us about economic worth and we did not listen to him.*

- *We had the man who put his life on the line for Jamaica and the people of Jamaica and we did not care for him.*

- *We had the man that sang to us about glory and truth; our pain and suffering and we did not listen to him. We allowed others to murder him.*

- *We had the name of Good God and Allelujah and we did vile and despicable things under his name.*

- *We had the doctor bird and sold it hence Air God - Air Jamaica is no more.*

- *We had paradise - Eden and we sold it to everyone and left our children futureless and homeless.*

All we asked for like I've said, Good God has and have given us but instead of listening and accepting his goodness and truth, we passed it up and handed self including country over to death.

Tell me how fair was that?

We cried wolf too much and now all the goodness of Good God has left us; passed us by.

We listened to others and played the fool; not only WRECKING SELF BUT WRECKING LAND - COUNTRY AND ECONOMY ALONG THE WAY AND OR IN THE PROCESS.

Instead of keeping our food organic we traded it for GENETICALLY MODIFIED CRAP THAT WE CALL FOOD and wonder why we have so much health issues on the island.

We should have never lost the flag of life but like Marcus Mosiah Garvey said, "A PEOPLE WITHOUT THE KNOWLEDGE OF THEIR PAST HISTORY, ORIGIN AND CULTURE IS LIKE A TREE WITHOUT ROOTS."

And he was infinitely and indefinitely correct; hence we did the things we did because we knew not our culture, heritage, language, origins. We knew not where we came from hence we lived like the dead and deceived each other.

WE KNEW NOT WHERE WE WERE GOING HENCE WE BECAME LOST; CHILDREN OF THE BROKEN AND LOST BEGGING FOR A BONE AT THEIR MASTER'S TABLE.

WE SAY AFRICA BUT YET KNOWETH NOT AFRICA.

WE SAY AFRICA BUT KNOWETH NOT THE ORIGINS OF AFRICA AND AFRICANS. HENCE WE KNEW NOT SELF.

TO YOU, ALL ARE AFRICANS IF YOU ARE BLACK AND FROM THE CONTINENT OF AFRICA, BUT YET DO NOT KNOW THAT THERE ARE BLACK BABYLONIANS THAT RESIDE IN INDIA UNTIL THIS DAY.

TO YOU ALL ARE AFRICANS IF YOU ARE BLACK AND FROM THE CONTINENT OF AFRICA, BUT KNOW NOT THAT MANY OF YOU ARE EUROPEANS, OF CHINESE ORIGINS.

TO YOU ALL ARE BLACK IF YOU ARE BLACK AND FROM THE CONTINENT FO AFRICA, BUT KNOWETH NOT THAT THE ORIGINAL CREATOR OF THE UNIVERSE AND EARTH IS BLACK. MEANING FALL UNDER THE BANNER OF BLACK, HENCE THE TRUE AND REAL JAMAICA FLAG - THE FLAG OF LIFE.

All this and more you do not know hence you know not of your genes in the physical and spiritual realm. All we gave up to be enslaved by people that had not our true and best interest at heart.

All black lands were infiltrated, hence all black lands were to fall and they did fall at the hands of evil. America is no different because America broke off South America and South America broke off Africa. Every land that is separated by oceans and seas broke away from THE CRADLE AND WOMB OF LIFE - AFRICA.

GOOD AND EVIL COULD NOT RESIDE TOGETHER HENCE THE SEPARATION IS NOT YET COMPLETE.

The process must be completed hence many lands will fall by the wayside due to their alliance and allegiance with Sin - Death. Yes the harvest comes and truly woe be unto man - humanity because many will feel it.

Africa was the hub and it's still the hub because in time Africa must reclaim her own and live in true peace.

Hence peace be still because death is coming to claim his and her own and Jamaica is no exception to the rule. They did not know that *"ALL ARE NOT AFRICANS AND NOT ALL BLACK PEOPLE FALL UNDER THE BANNER OF BLACK - GOOD GOD." Hence a nation that knoweth not their true culture, heritage and language including their own (people) are like trees without roots - dead.*

As Jamaicans we fail to recognize the truth hence we pree death and death's own; people.

Someone gives you a nasty book and say it is of God, unnu jump up an sey a di truth an a so eee go. But yet ask you about your true roots, culture and heritage and you cannot tell me or anyone.

Ask you about what God – Good God look like and you cannot tell me.

Ask you where you came from and or belong in Africa and you cannot tell me. But instead you will lie to me and tell me "White people enslaved your ancestors and took them out of Africa."

Not one of you can stand to hear the truth because no one took us out of Africa unwillingly.

WE SOLD OUT GOOD GOD AND ALLELUJAH BY JOINING FORCES WITH EVIL HENCE SELLING HIM AND OUR OWN TO THE HIGHEST BIDDER.

If Africans were true they would tell the truth because the first country to disgrace and discredit Good God for a place in hell, were the nasty Ethiopians that some of you so worship and praise. Hence many of you wave the Ethiopian flag and think you are doing something good when you are not. You are praising and worshiping death as well as bringing death and destruction upon you and your land. Yes this takes time meaning over time hence Jamaica will feel it shortly because they did worse than the lots of you literally.

Ethiopia has never done anything good for the black civilization hence Nimrod the Black Babylonian deceived many and married his own mother. So truly look back at our so called ancestral history and know the truth. You do not need books of men to lie to you all you have to do is live clean and ask Good God for the truth. He will show you everything from the conception of time until this day and beyond.

We are the ones like I've said that don't want to know the truth. We would rather live in lies and teach lies rather than hear the truth and know the truth.

So if we know not the truth and live by the truth we cannot have life nor have everlasting life.

Yes every nation has their nasty history but we did not have to live this way.

We live like crab inna barrel and wonder why we are suffering.

We cannot stand to see our own rise up because to some of you, that person do not deserve it. But who are you to say he or she does not deserve happiness, financial wealth, a good education, medical help and so forth? He or she has worked so damn hard to achieve his or her own and you do all to cut them down. You don't want them to succeed like Good God and Allelujah gave you all.

That person worked hard let him or her be.

Good God gave us his knowledge by calling his chosen few but you cut them down and say they don't deserve Good God and Allelujah so you do all to discredit that person. Live clean and he Good God and Allelujah will call you to his duty and or service. Come on now.

Stop the obeah working and nastiness and repent and you will see how your life lift up over time. I say over time because you now have to prove to him Good God and Allelujah that you are worthy and trustworthy. Jamaica made a pledge and could not honour it, so now Jamaica and Jamaicans have to redeem self and show Good God and Allelujah that he can trust them.

Like I've said, it did not have to be this way hence we were not trustworthy in the beginning. So because of trust he could not stay with us and no matter how he's tried with us we continue to fail him.

A true messenger of Good God and Allelujah do not want your financial wealth and prosperity. They truly want and need what's best for land and people including you.

They don't want you to go to hell hence sometimes they put their lives on the line for you and this is sad. Like I've said, in a couple of my other books; I cannot afford to piss off death anymore. I have to let Jamaica and its people go because death will plow me down - take my life if I continue to interfere in what is rightfully theirs. Yes to a large extent this is how some of the messengers of Good God dies. We've tried and delivered the message that was given to us, it is up to the people of the land to accept the message or reject it. You as a messenger did your job and it's now up to the people to truly go to Good God and let him confirm the message because you as a messenger cannot. Yes many people say they don't believe in dreams but that is their right hence many of them miss the message and die shortly afterwards. True council and goodness cannot lie hence know the truth of Good God and Allelujah. I cannot see everything but what I see I tell you because that was what I saw.

Yes sometimes I want to break my vow to him because the road I walk is lonely and tough and I tell him this. Hence learn to talk to Good God and Allelujah because he does listen to you.

You have to trust him in all that you do and trust me it's not easy to do this. It is hard hence take your time and think of the consequences before you sin.

Every sin has a weight and or consequences and what you do not want for self do not want or need it for others.

As Jamaican many of us do not know due to ignorance that some White and Chinese fall under the banner of black and are truly protected under this banner; hence the Jamaican Motto, "OUT OF MANY ONE PEOPLE."

I tried Jamaica, I tried but my tears and plea was not good enough. I've cried for you and vomited in the process.

I've stayed death for you and death was upset - angry at me.

I've written harsh words for you to hear me and change your dirty linen of self and clothing but was stopped from reaching you.

I've talked and quarrel with Good God but I can no longer tear down his walls to try and save you.

I truly love you but I HAVE TO LEARN THAT UNCLEAN IS UNCLEAN AND GOOD GOD HAS AND HAVE DEEMED YOU AS A NATION, LAND AND PEOPLE UNCLEAN AND I HAVE TO ABIDE BY THIS. I CAN NO LONGER BREAK HIM DOWN WHEN IT COMES TO YOU.

It's unfortunate things have to be this way but we as a people are stiff necked, stubborn and untrue when it comes to goodness - Good God. Hence we could not honour our pledge to him before man, him and the universe including earth.

We lied to him hence he cannot trust us nor can I because none can honour our word - the national pledge.

WE GAVE GOOD GOD AND ALLELUJAH OUR WORD BUT IN THE END, ENDED UP LYING TO HIM AND SELF.

We have no honour because if we did Jamaica would not be unclean. He Good God would not tell me Jamaica is unclean. He Good God would not stop me from going into the island if the island was clean.

GOOD GOD DEALS IN CLEAN AND IF YOU ARE NOT CLEAN - TRYING TO BE CLEAN, HE CANNOT BE WITH YOU.

HE CANNOT ASK YOU TO DO ANYTHING FOR HIM IF YOU ARE UNCLEAN AND UNTRUSTWORTHY.

Yes Jamaica I truly love you with a good and true heart but in all my truth I could not save you. I truly cannot go against Good God for you or anyone because in the end, I have a soul and spirit that is truly important to me. And yes although Good God has and have deemed Jamaica unclean and the flag of life has been handed over to death, I have to take the flag of life back from death because this flag does not belong to death. This flag truly belongs to life - Good God.

THE FLAG OF LIFE IS A SOUTHERN FLAG AND NOT A NORTHERN ONE, HENCE THE CHILDREN OF GOD - GOOD GOD FLY HIS FLAGS HIGH AND PROUD.

We know the truth of the South hence we are Southern Bells. We loathe strive, fighting and all that is unclean - sinful.

Yes the South has done its share of wrongs but the SOUTHERN LANDS MUST CLEAN THEMSELVES UP AND WALK AWAY FOR ALL THAT IS EVIL.

Hence Good God I come to you for truth and honesty. I come to you with my good will of truth and justice in all that is pure and just to end the feud.

Satan lost in 1313(2013) hence the North can no longer control it all.

The fighting between NORTH AND SOUTH must now end.

Truly no more Good God because many lives have been lost on both sides.

I cannot take the strife and evils anymore. Sin must now stop and be stopped because what sin did to man - humanity was not right nor was it just. You cannot take someone to hell with you just because you lost and or don't like them.

You cannot give unclean meat to humanity to eat and say it is good food. This is wrong come on now.

Wrong is wrong Good God and you now know that Good cannot live with evil hence North cannot co-exist in true peace and harmony with South.

North will always want control and this is not right. No one should control anyone hence infinitely and indefinitely never ever rise up the East to fight against the West.

It's too much Good God, truly too much. The pain and hurt is too great hence I am pleading with you in goodness and truth to stop this feud - war between North and South.

Separate the two (Good and Evil) and let sin and death go their own way in true peace - truth indefinitely and forever ever.

Life - Good and True Life is worth it hence squash this.

Lives were taken and both sides are wrong. Neither North and South is just because in truth, no one should fight and or create strife to control and dominate anyone. We should know that the more we kill and create strife amongst each other the more death comes.

Strife is a sin because strife is hate.

Killing is a sin because killing takes the flesh; that which houses the spirit. Hence the flesh is the house and or home of the spirit.

Jamaica I truly cried for you hence I am truly sorry I could not save you.

Truly listen to Jodeci's Cry For You because like I said, I did cry for you. I truly wanted to save you - land and good people but not wicked and sinful people.

Time did tell because Bob Marley, Marcus Garvey and others did tell - warn and none of you listened.

Right now Jamaica is broken and needs healing. Truly listen to Byron Cage's Broken But I Am Healed. Maybe after hearing this song you will receive your blessings and change the dirty linen of self and country.

KNOW THAT DESPITE MY TRUST ISSUES OF YOU, IF GOOD GOD SAY ONE DAY, MICHELLE THE PEOPLE OF JAMAICA INCLUDING LAND HAVE AND HAS RETURNED TO ME AND THEY ARE NOW INFINITELY AND INFINITELY CLEAN, YOU CAN BUILD MY HOUSE ON THE LAND I WILL NOT REFUSE HIM. I HAVE TO LISTEN TO HIM AND BUILD HIS HOUSE IN YOU AND ON YOUR LAND.

You have to change now and set yourself free from Satan and death. Listen to the song because it said,

"God can heal, he can deliver. He can mend your brokenness. He has a miracle to fit your needs. Once you trust him you will receive."

All you have to do is receive him in truth and truly praise him.

You need to be honest and with him Good God.

You need to go to him Good God in truth and honesty and tell him that you did not know because certain things you did not know.

Know that God - Good God is the healer and the fixer and he can and will fix you perfectly if you are truly true to him - trust him.

He cannot let you down if you are good and true because *TRUTH WILL FOREVER EVER BE EVERLASTING LIFE.*

Goodness cannot die all it can do is grow. So truly trust Good God and let him truly help you to fix self and Jamaica - country.

Reclaim your life because even though I said once Good God has deemed you unclean you can never get him back you can if you are truthful to him. Forgiveness is there but not all can be forgiven. Disobedience cannot be forgiven because this sin is against Good God so truly know your sins and what you are asking forgiveness for.

Do not think of Evening (Eve) and our ancestors of old. Think of you and your soul as well as your children and family's souls.

Yes we made Jamaica unclean but cleanliness is there. Like I've told you in another book, Jamaica must come back 99.9 percent clean. (And please do not bring 666 into this because it is so not warranted). Lysol in the yellow bottle is what you Jamaicans need to clean your home and self. So truly clean you and receive your healing and blessings.

I am not Good God, hence try because I too signed against him and look there, I am writing for him.

Truly trust him even though the hour seems hopeless and dark. Trust me it's not dark hence I gave him back the Flag of Life. Yes death must take who belongs to him but if you do not belong to death, death cannot take you.

So hold your hand up to glory and listen. Stop being stiff necked and stubborn. *Please this is your life so accept life and now live by your pledge because this pledge is extremely important.*

The fire of hell is hotter than the sun and like I've told you in my other books, the spirit is the one to feel pain. The sun of the earth cannot kill the spirit because this sun is not ATOMIC FIRE as I call it. So truly save you.

Please, if you truly love Good God then live because you are worth it. Many of you know what I am talking about so truly turn from your evil ways. I am pleading with you.

EVERY BLACK CHILD AND OR PERSON GOOD GOD LOSES TO EVIL IS A VICTORY FOR DEATH AND WE CAN NO LONGER GIVE DEATH THE VICTORY OVER US.

Do not continue to lose your life because of others - the lies that they tell you.

WE DID NOT ACCEPT MOSES HENCE MOSES HAD TO TAKE LIFE OUT OF EGYPT AND BRING IT INTO CHINA. HENCE THE CHINESE KEPT THE YING AND YANG UNTIL THIS DAY. They know how important this life is but yet greed has taken hold of some because of ethics and human rights issues. But they will have to smarten up shortly because the two sisters of prosperity are that strict when it comes to respect. _Trust me they can and will take the PROSPERITY OF CHINA IF CHINA DOES NOT SMARTEN UP._

It's a waiting game now hence China you are duly warned. You cannot accept life and treat your people with disrespect.

You cannot accept life and China has so much smog.

Greed is not the issue hence do what you can to clean up your country in a positive and good way.

Truly do not become like the 90 percent of humanity because this destruction is a global destruction and your country is no exception to the law and laws of life and death.

Many things you know hence I truly have to leave you alone.

You accepted life but the hatred and killings must stop because war is not the answer. Hence truly trust life because you have life.

__We as blacks keep getting a chance at life and we keep refusing it hence life keep passing us by.__

SO TO AFRICA, JAMAICA ALL THE BLACK LANDS OF THIS EARTH INCLUDING ALL THE SOUTHERN LANDS, TRULY LISTEN AND RECEIVE YOUR BLESSINGS.

As southern beings you can no longer walk in the foundations and evils of the North because the North has nothing to do with us. Pray sincerely to self and Good God daily and ask him to protect your land and people. Know that we must do this together in unison so that WHEN DEATH COMES YOU ARE SAVED. And as always no Jesus because Jesus did not exist. God, Good God, Allelujah and if he Good God is Lovey to you then Lovey is fine and appropriate to use in your prayers.

Allelujah will be funny to use because we are not accustomed to calling him Good God this. We only cry this name out when the spirit feels his energy flowing through us.

So if you don't feel comfortable in using Allelujah that's fine because I can't fully call God - Good God Allelujah on a daily basis but I'm learning now.

Life is worth it Jamaica. So do all you can to help you because things are going to get worse shortly and no one can blame anyone for this. Jamaica must blame Jamaica because as people you keep voting people into office that are corrupt. They have not the best interest of Jamaica at heart and now Jamaica is on the chopping block of death literally.

You have to wake up because your time is winding down.

Michelle Jean

OTHER BOOKS BY MICHELLE JEAN

Blackman Redemption - The Fall of Michelle Jean

Blackman Redemption - After the Fall Apology

Blackman Redemption - World Cry - Christine Lewis

Blackman Redemption

Blackman Redemption - The Rise and Fall of Jamaica

Blackman Redemption - The War of Israel

Blackman Redemption - The Way I Speak to God

Blackman Redemption - A Little Talk With Man

Blackman Redemption - The Den of Thieves

Blackman Redemption - The Death of Jamaica

Blackman Redemption - Happy Mother's Day

Blackman Redemption - The Death of Faith

Blackman Redemption - The War of Religion

Blackman Redemption - The Death of Russia

Blackman Redemption - The Truth

Blackman Redemption - Spiritual War

The New Book of Life

The New Book of Life - A Cry For The Children

The New Book of Life – Judgement
The New Book of Life – Love Bound
The New Book of Life – Me
The New Book of Life – Life

Just One of Those Days
Book Two – Just One of Those Days
Just One of Those Days – Book Three The Way I
Feel
Just One of Those Days – Book Four

The Days I Am Weak
Crazy Thoughts – My Book of Sin
Broken
Ode to Mr. Dean Fraser

A Little Little Talk
A Little Little Talk – Book Two

Prayers
My Collective
A Little Talk/A Time For Fun and Play
Simple Poems
Behind The Scars
Songs of Praise And Love

Love Bound
Love Bound – Book Two

Dedication Unto My Kids
More Talk
Saving America From A Woman's Perspective
My Collective the Other Side of Me
My Collective the Dark Side of Me
A Blessed Day
Lose To Win
My Doubtful Days - Book One

My Little Talk With God
My Little Talk With God - Book Two

A Different Mood and World - Thinking

My Nagging Day
My Nagging Day - Book Two

Friday September 13, 2013
My True Love
It Would Be You
My Day

A Little Advice - Talk
1313, 2032, 2132 - The End of Man
Tata

MICHELLE'S BOOK BLOG - BOOKS 1 - 16

My Problem Day
A Better Way
Stay - Adultery and the Weight of Sin -
Cleanliness Message

Let's Talk
Lonely Days - Foundation